CHRISTIAN FOLK ART

by

Ann Elliott

Step-by-Step Methods to Convey
Messages of Faith, Hope, Love,
and the Way of the Cross

The draw, paint, cutout, and shape methods in this book cost
little or nothing to make. They are forms of creative expression
anyone—young and old alike—can do. Moreover, the special,
seasonal projects included offer specific ways of returning to the
age-old folk custom of instilling spiritual meaning into the work
of the hands—"And in his handicraft shall be his prayer," Eccle-
siaticus 38:39.

Morehouse-Barlow Co., Inc.
Wilton, Connecticut

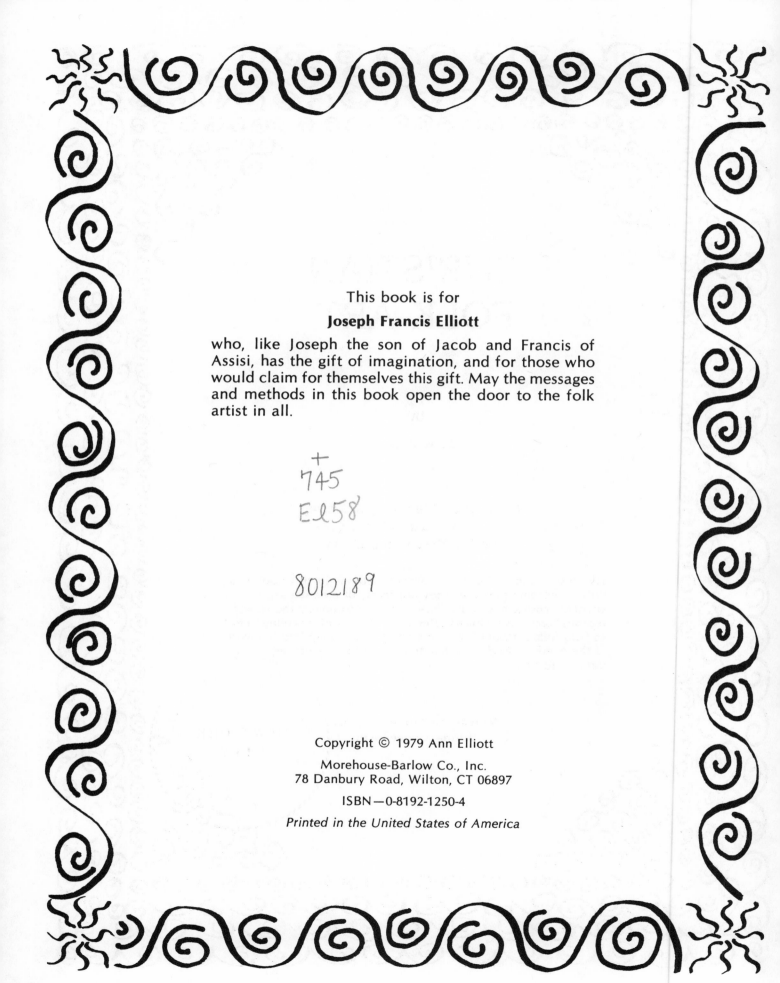

This book is for

Joseph Francis Elliott

who, like Joseph the son of Jacob and Francis of Assisi, has the gift of imagination, and for those who would claim for themselves this gift. May the messages and methods in this book open the door to the folk artist in all.

Copyright © 1979 Ann Elliott

Morehouse-Barlow Co., Inc.
78 Danbury Road, Wilton, CT 06897

ISBN—0-8192-1250-4

Printed in the United States of America

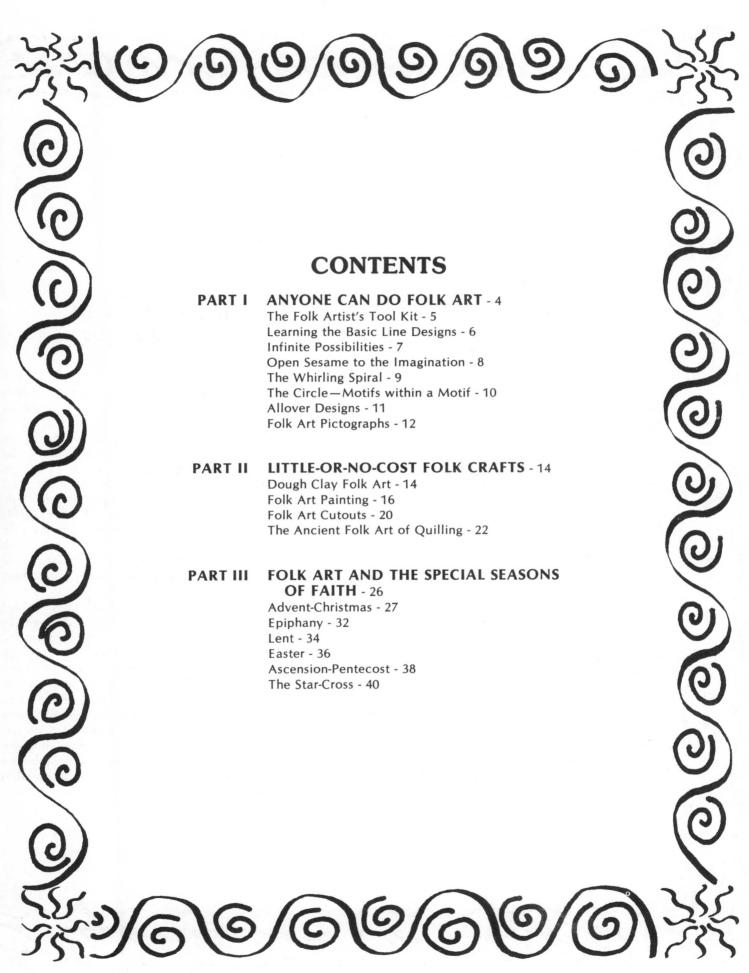

CONTENTS

Part I — Introduction

ANYONE CAN DO FOLK ART AND HAVE IT BE AS FULL OF MEANING AS IT IS DECORATIVE!

This book began several years ago on a rainy winter day when our youngest son, Joseph, came into the kitchen where I stood at the sink preparing vegetables for a pot of soup. Plopping himself down at the table, he complained: "I'm bored. What can I do?"

"How would you like to learn Folk Art?" I asked. I was remembering when his three older brothers and two older sisters had been his age. This method had sparked their creative imaginations and kept them busy for hours on end.

"Folk Art?" a now curious Joseph questioned. "What's that?"

"Do you remember those bird decorations which we hang on the tree every Christmas?"

"The ones the brothers and sisters made?" he questioned, eyes brightening now.

"Mmmmhum. The very ones. Well, the designs of those shapes are Folk Art. How would you like to learn about them?"

"I sure would!"

And so Joseph, now nine years old, began learning the age-old, ageless way of adding color and interest to just about anything and everything. Since that rainy day, he has frequently come to me with "I'm bored," yet been quick to add, "Teach me something *new* about Folk Art." Whenever possible I have taken a few minutes from whatever I have been doing to give him a new idea in the form of an exercise or project. It never seemed to take much of my time to ignite his enthusiasm.

This book is the result of Joseph's persistence, as, little by little, it has grown from its beginning. The method is presented here pretty much as Joseph learned it—step-by-step. I noted that at the point I began running out of "something new" to teach him, he began getting ideas of his own. For example, his 20th-century, young mind is fascinated currently with geodesic domes and other many-faceted shapes. With the help of his older brother, Conal, he has made several different models of these and decorated them with folk art motifs.

This is a good example of how Folk Art has evolved through the ages: familiar and utilitarian shapes have been enriched with Folk Art designs. And, interesting to note for our purposes, those decorations, although varying in style and arrangement, consistently have been composed of the same basic elements of design.

As a design-student many years ago, I learned that these motifs of ancient and modern design are few in number. They can, in fact, be reduced to two—dot and line. However, for the sake of stimulating the imagination, I like to think of them as numbering eight, and of forming a "Tool Kit" to carry around in my head wherever I go.

THE FOLK ARTIST'S TOOL KIT

Learning these eight age-old elements of Folk Art was Joseph's first lesson. I suggested he think of a tool kit with four small compartments, the first containing a dot and a line;

The second compartment containing two "running" motifs, a wavy line and a zigzag line;

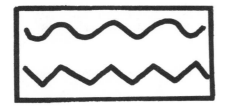

The third section of the tool kit, three basic shapes, the circle, the square and the triangle;

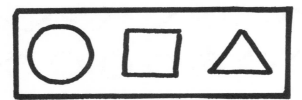

The fourth place, a very special motif (the whirling spiral upon which entire art and craft forms are based—decorative ironwork, intricate gold and silver jewelry) and an ancient paper folk craft called "quilling."

STEP-BY-STEP EXERCISES FOR LEARNING THE BASIC LINE DESIGNS OF ALL FOLK ART— ANCIENT AND NEW

These first two exercises are for the purpose of learning the eight basic motifs and of learning firsthand how simple it is to construct decorative borders. You will need a black felt pen or crayon, plain white paper, a pencil, and a ruler.

Exercise #1—Borders *Step One:* Lightly pencil in nine spaces ½" apart. *Step Two:* Fill in each space with one of the motifs, as shown below. *Step Three:* Repeat *Step One,* arranging the motifs in different orders. Already, you begin to see the varied effects from the same motifs.

Exercise #2—Frames *Step One:* Lightly pencil 4 or more ¼" spaces around the edges of a sheet of paper. *Step Two:* Fill in each space with one of the motifs, as shown bordering this page.

ON THE INFINITE POSSIBILITIES OF CREATING FOLK ART DESIGNS

My son Conal, a mathematics major, did some calculations: Based on the eight tool-kit folk art motifs, there are 28 possible combinations of any two of the motifs—all different. If, instead of combining two motifs, three different ones are used together, then there are 56 combination possibilities; combining four motifs, there are 70 possible combinations. And, progressing through combinations of five, six and seven, there are, all together, 247 possibilities for combining two or more of these eight motifs. Nor does it end there, for, by differing the size of the motifs, or by arranging them in clusters, or turning them in different directions, the possibilities for creating different designs becomes almost infinite.

In the exercises below and on the next few pages are some examples—a mere as-a drop-of-water-is-to-the-ocean sampling.

Exercise #3—As in Exercises #1 and #2, mark off spaces and make borders and frames, this time combining two or more of the motifs in each space.

OPEN SESAME TO THE IMAGINATION

In addition to the eight motifs, four magic words belong in the Folk Artist's Tool Kit. They are the keys for unlocking the doors to the imaginative faculties. Held in mind, these words are your encouragement to be inventive, to experiment, and to improvise as you go along.

COMBINE
VARY
GROUP
ROTATE

Exercise #4   *Step One:* Try varying the size of a motif, repeating the variation, then slanting it in a different direction.

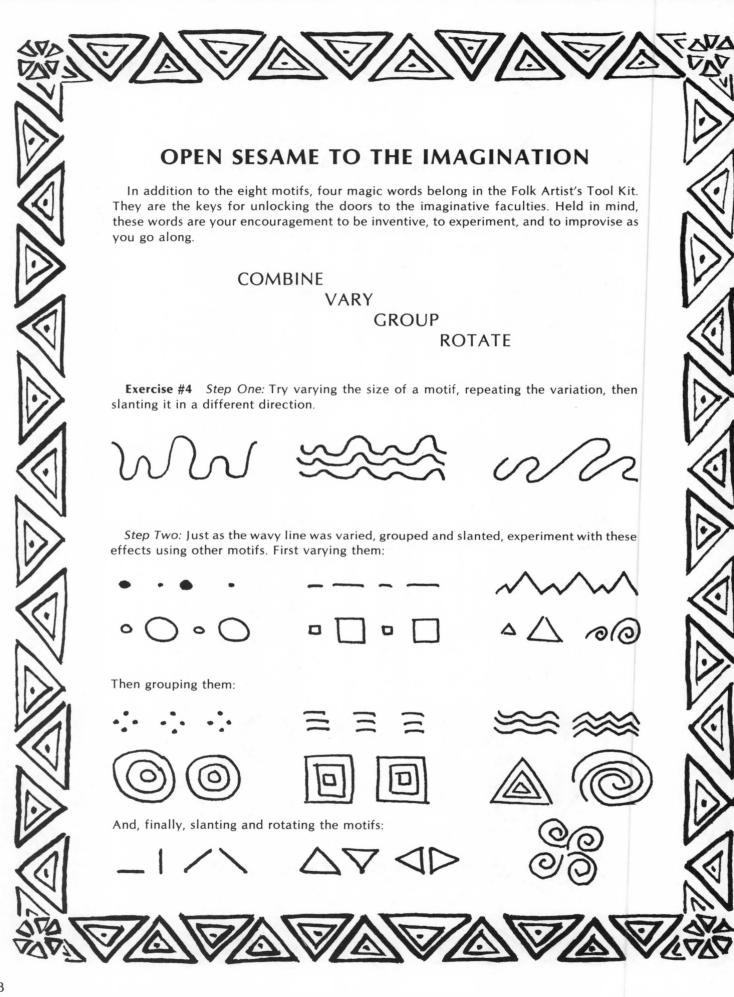

Step Two: Just as the wavy line was varied, grouped and slanted, experiment with these effects using other motifs. First varying them:

Then grouping them:

And, finally, slanting and rotating the motifs:

THE WHIRLING SPIRAL

From the nebulae of outer space to the house of the lowly snail, the spiral would seem to contain some of nature's most dynamic secrets. This motif has a number of basic variations. By combining, varying, grouping and rotating just the eight shown below, it would be possible to keep on making snowflake and flower designs without ever making the same one twice. These whirling spiral variations also can be observed to be the basis of most ornamental iron work as well as that of much gold and silver handmade jewelry. They are also the basis of an ancient folk art called *Quilling* which is one of the folk art methods detailed on later pages. The descriptive names of the variations shown below are: a - the spiral; b - the **S** scroll; c - the curved scroll; d - the heart scroll; e - the closed **v**; f - the open **v**; g - the wave scroll; and h - the quote scroll.

Exercise #5—Using the spiral and its variations, make border or frame designs (1-3 examples below). As another part of this exercise, arrange variations of the spiral around centers into flower motifs (examples 4-6).

THE CIRCLE—MOTIFS WITHIN A MOTIF

The circle could be called the master nature-motif—so many are the natural forms whose lines are circular or are the curved parts of the circle. In nature, the circle represents the sun; in religious symbolism, it stands for the eternal beginning-without-end nature of God. It is of little wonder that ancient peoples looked upon the circle-shaped sun as "the one god," or that Malachi, the last book of the Old Testament, ends with a promise of the coming "Sun of Righteousness." In making folk art designs, the motifs within the circle create a great many more possibilities. Several ways of dividing a circle are shown below: a - the horizontal half-circle or curved line; b - vertical half-circle; c - rotated curved lines; d and e - two curved lines joined into **S** curves; f - intersecting circles; g - the crescent and leaf or eye shapes formed by the intersecting of two circles.

Exercise #6—Below are some examples of representational forms drawn with the above circle-based motifs. Use these in composing frame and border designs and, then, in making the Allover Designs (**Exercise #7**) and the Pictographs (**Exercise #8**) on the following pages.

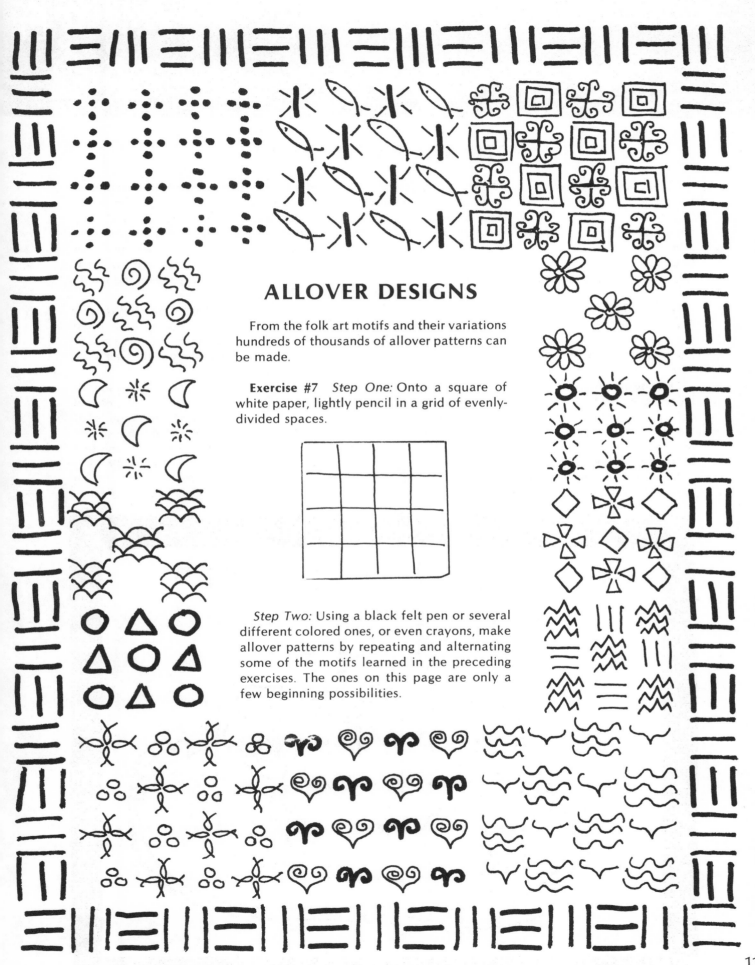

ALLOVER DESIGNS

From the folk art motifs and their variations hundreds of thousands of allover patterns can be made.

Exercise #7 *Step One:* Onto a square of white paper, lightly pencil in a grid of evenly-divided spaces.

Step Two: Using a black felt pen or several different colored ones, or even crayons, make allover patterns by repeating and alternating some of the motifs learned in the preceding exercises. The ones on this page are only a few beginning possibilities.

FOLK ART PICTOGRAPHS

To get Joseph started making Folk Art Pictographs, the name given to some very early examples of primitive folk art, I gave him a series of "assignments"—the ones included in **Exercise #8** below. And to brighten up his results, I provided four felt pens—red, yellow, green, and blue. We had talked already about the secrets of the circle and all the nature forms to be made from it. We had seen also how mountains could be made from zigzag lines, and that, from squares and triangles, houses and other buildings could be made, and, how folk art stick figures of persons and animals (similar to the drawings at the top of this page) could be made. Most of this wasn't new to Joseph, but it encouraged him to include in his Folk Artist's Tool Kit the way of drawing that comes naturally to a child.

After Joseph had finished his "assignments" and begged to do still more folk art, I suggested that he make up little stories to go along with his drawings, stories that told of the wonders of creation, or whatever his own imagination told him, while he drew. This telling oneself a story to go along with the work of one's hands is very typical of the folk artist's way of working. It is also the way folk artists instill their work with symbolic meaning and spiritual relevance.

Exercise #8   *Joseph's Pictograph Assignments*—Use a separate piece of paper for each of the following Pictographs: (1) Using circles and parts of circles make a "garden" of flowers of different shapes and colors; (2) Using curved lines and straight lines make a "forest" of trees—beginning with the examples at the top of this page and then inventing other ways of showing trees; (3) Make a picture of a house and decorate it with folk art motifs; (4) Make another house and then add to your picture 2 trees, 3 clouds, 4 birds, and 5 flowers; (5) Make a water picture with waves, a boat, lots of fish, a sun, birds and clouds.

My own favorite Pictograph subjects are from the Scriptures. Psalm 148 is illustrated on the facing page. For those who embroider or do applique work, Pictographs are easy to make and use as patterns.

Praise
the Lord!
all his
angels
Praise him
sun + moon
shining stars
Praise him
highest heaven
and waters
above the
heavens
Praise the
Lord!
from the
earth
sea monsters
and all deeps
fire
snow
stormy wind
mountains
and all hills
fruit trees
and all
cedars
beasts and
all cattle
creeping
things
and flying
birds
all peoples
Praise
the Lord!
Psalm 148

Part II

LITTLE-OR-NO-COST FOLK ART CRAFTS

Folk art is defined as the handiwork of untrained, ordinary people who choose this form of creative expression as a pastime and to add color to their everyday lives. They paint whatever is at hand: furniture, window boxes, all manner of household accessories. Nor is the folk artist's decoration limited to painting household furnishings. Colorful designs are also woven, carved, modeled, or embroidered. The colors are as bright and rich as possible—reds, yellows, blues, and greens. But the subject matter of the designs used are chosen for a different than decorative purpose. They are chosen for their tradition-based, symbolic value. At least, this was so in less materially-minded times. However, even when symbolic meanings are lost for a time they are still there to be rediscovered. That is what we are doing in these exercises and projects. Symbolic understanding and creativity go hand in hand and are at the heart of the folk person's art as a particular design is innovated and given a spontaneity which characterizes this art's naivety, or childlike quality.

On this and the next few pages are four folk art crafts. These particular crafts are chosen because they leave the kind of room for individual creativity that is needed if the true spirit of folk art is to be pursued.

Dough Clay for Folk Art

Although the ingredients of this folk craft are humble, the results can be beautiful and durable. For minimal costs, you can make folk decorations, gifts, and even works of art. It is good today for hours of purposeful "rainy-day" recreation, and as the base for making symbolically-meaningful folk art objects.

Below are two clays made from ingredients out of the kitchen cupboard. Like clays that come out of the ground, each of these produces a different effect.

Flour Clay: 3 cups all purpose flour; 1 cup salt; 1 cup water (more or less).

Step One: Add water to dry ingredients, little by little, until the dough holds together without being crumbly or sticky. Add more flour or water, accordingly. Knead for five to ten minutes to form a ball of dough that is free from lumps.

Step Two: Roll out onto well-floured board to ½" thickness.

Step Three: Place a pattern cut from paper on top of the dough. With the point of a knife, cut around the pattern. Smooth around the edges with a wet knife or finger. Insert a paper clip or hairpin into the top for a hanger.

Step Four: (Optional) Using tools from kitchen, desk, or workbench, impress folk art motifs into the clay. For the fish, lines can be made with the side and tip of a knitting needle; curved and wavy lines with the side of a ring; small curved lines with the top of a paper clip. Or, as in the border of this page, dots can be made with nail heads and dashes with the tip of a screwdriver. Zigzags can be made with the tip of a "church key" can opener.

Step Five: Air-dry overnight or longer on a wire rack. After the top surface is well-hardened, turn the object over and continue until drying is complete. Or, after partially drying, place the shape on a tinfoil-lined cookie sheet and bake in a slow oven (300° or less) for an hour or longer, until the shape feels hard and dry. The drier the object is before baking, and the more slowly it is baked, the better are the results.

Step Six: (Optional) For an allover golden color, brush the top of the shape with beaten egg, evaporated milk, or a mixture of both during the last 15 or 30 minutes of baking: For a light-golden finish, brush once; for a darker appearance, brush twice.

Step Seven: Remove the object from the oven and cool. It can be left natural, painted according to the directions on pages 16–18, or, if it has been impressed with designs as suggested in *Step Four* (above), it can be "antiqued" as follows: Paint the front and back of the object with black or brown acrylic paint (see pages 16–18), or choose a bright color and darken it with an equal portion of black paint. When this dries, choose a bright color or gold or silver paint and dry-brush this over the top. To dry-brush, dip a dry brush into thick paint, then wipe off the excess. By dragging the side of the brush over the top, the indented impressions are left dark and give an "antiqued" look. This method allows room for experimenting with different effects.

Step Eight: Unless the object has been painted on all sides with an acrylic or oil base paint, it will need a final coat of varnish or shellac applied to all sides. This will protect it from moisture and future deterioration, making a very permanent object from such ordinary ingredients.

Cornmeal Clay: 2 cups cornmeal; 1 cup salt; 1 to 1¼ cups water.

Follow the flour clay steps with these exceptions: (1) This dough can be rolled more thinly, ¼" or less, (2) It can be air dried as in *Step Five* above. If you are anxious to get on with the project, it can be baked immediately in a *very* slow oven (250° or less) until dry and hard but not browned. This produces a background approximately the color and warmth of wood and makes a highly complimentary surface for painting on brightly-colored motifs.

The Fish shown on the facing page can be traced around and used as a Dough Clay pattern. Before rolling out the clay, make paper copies of the bare shape and experiment decorating the shape by combining, varying, grouping and rotating different "Tool Kit" motifs. (Review page 8.) Then proceed with the above directions. If you want to make imprints in the wet clay, follow *Step Four*.

The Fish was the secret sign that early, persecuted Christians used to identify themselves to one another. Jesus' disciples were fishermen whom he called to be "fishers of men." He also fed the multitude by multiplying the loaves and fishes. The Greek letters IXOUS spell *fish* and also are the first Greek letters of the following words: I—Jesus; X—Christ; O—of God; U—Son; S—Savior.

FOLK ART PAINTING

When the Pennsylvania "Dutch" came to America from their 100-plus-30-year war-torn, plague-ravished Germany *(Deutsch)* homeland, many brought with them only one change of clothes, what few essential tools they could carry, and their Bibles. In their memories, however, they brought also centuries-old European folk art motifs. Flowers, hearts and birds were among their favorite motifs, and, according to a leading authority on these original Pennsylvania settlers, their designs were religiously inspired.

The **Heart** was used dominately to decorate birth-and-baptism certificates and to enclose scriptural texts. It was not used as a sentimental symbol, but as a reminder of the heart of God, the *source* of love. Heart = Love.

Flowers, in particular those that came from bulbs — flowering, dying, and flowering again — symbolized the scriptural promise of eternal life. This was their hope. Flowers = Hope.

Particular meanings were attributed to **Birds** of different species, while birds, in general, symbolized humanity's higher aspirations and faith in God. Birds = Faith.

The **Rooster's** popularity as a folk symbol was widespread throughout Europe and Early America. This domestic bird was said to have had contemplative value for Western Europe's cloistered orders because of the scriptural reference, in Matthew 26:34, to Peter's denial of Jesus — a poignant reminder of human vulnerability and one's awakening to the need for Grace if one is to remain *faithful* to the Lord. The contemporary Cursillo Movement has adopted the rooster as its symbol — the "many colors" of the rooster denoting the resultant joys and blessings as faith in Christ deepens.

Birds, Flowers, Hearts — Faith, Hope, Love. This is the traditional, symbolic message the folk artist re-interprets and passes along to succeeding generations.

Easy-to-Learn Folk Art Painting Exercises

In the painting corner of the Folk Artist's Tool Kit are three essential brush strokes; the Straight Stroke, the Comma Stroke, and the **S** Stroke — each having particular decorative uses. Combine these with dots, circles, curved and straight lines and you, too, are set to reaffirm in color and symbol the message of the Gospel — Faith, Hope and Love.

Mastering the strokes is very simple. It just takes a little practice — as with a child first learning to print and then to do cursive writing. As you practice these strokes, you will observe that the more quickly and naturally you make them, the more expressive and graceful they will look. If you don't get the knack of it at first, don't give up. You'll catch on with a little more practice. I promise.

You will need: a round, tapering-to-a-point brush. A good quality, red sable watercolor brush is the type most often recommended. Begin with a size six or eight and add smaller and larger sizes later. For practice paint, you can mix a few drops of food coloring with a small amount of evaporated or regular milk. For a palette, a white plate will do, and, for paper, any you have on hand.

The Straight Stroke: Begin by dipping your brush into the paint. Twist the brush slightly against the edge of the palette to shape the tip. Assuming you are sitting at a table, hold your hand at nearly a right angle to the paper. Steady your wrist or forearm against the edge of the table and/or the tip of your little finger. Now, touch the paper with the tip of the brush and begin bearing down on the brush and pulling it towards you. Then, *gradually*, lift the brush up, finishing the stroke to a point as the tip of the brush leaves the paper. Try making this stroke from different angles and with two coming together into a heart-shape. Also, practice running this stroke in a continuous horizontal line, rhythmically lifting and applying pressure to the brush (as at the top of the opposite page). Use this stroke, also, for making leaf borders (as at the bottom right of the opposite page). With this same stroke, make daisies (as shown at the very bottom left of this page).

The Comma Stroke: This stroke is made with the same bearing-and-lifting pressure as the above stroke with this exception—curve the stroke, as in making a comma, as you pull it towards you and lift the brush to a point. With this stroke you can make droopy-petaled flowers and leaves (as below and at the very bottom right). You can also make fatter hearts (below) and borders (middle design at top of opposite page and center bottom, also opposite page).

The S Stroke: Make this stroke the same as the above strokes, except begin more slowly, tipping the top of the stroke while pulling it forward and lifting it to form an **S** curve. This stroke makes tulips (center, bottom) and curved **S** leaves and borders (top and bottom of opposite page). It also makes little birds of no particular variety.

FOLK ART PAINTING PROJECTS

For durable projects, acrylic paints are the easiest ones with which to work. They are water soluable until dry, then permanent. They come in boxes of small-sized tubes of assorted colors or in single, larger-sized tubes. A box of small, assorted tubes, plus a large tub of white, will last a long time and do a whole lot of folk art. They are available wherever school, art, or paint supplies are sold.

You probably already have items suitable for folk-art decorating projects—clay flowerpots, old trays, wooden toys, tin buckets, cans, cannisters, boxes, lamp bases, bird houses, bookends, garden tool handles, watering cans, wooden spoons and bowls, picture frames, even larger items such as an old chest of drawers, a desk, chair, or even the kitchen cupboards. The Pennsylvania Dutch relied on folk-art decorated boxes for their apple-pie-order housekeeping. They had boxes for candles, for darning, for toys, and even for raising their bread dough. If you have an old wooden or metal recipe box, you can make it decorative while practicing folk art painting.

Preparing Items for Decorating: Any of the above or other items should first be prepared as for any other painting project: by cleaning, filling holes and sanding if necessary, and then painting on one or more base coats. Partially-used cans of oil or latex flat enamel paint, left over from house-painting projects can be used. Apply base coats with whatever appropriately-sized brush you have on hand. Metal objects first need to be washed in equal parts of vinegar and water to help the paint adhere. For small projects, I use a few squeezes from my large tub of white acrylic for undercoating.

Adding the Designs: Onto the prepared, undercoated surface, lightly pencil on folk-art motifs—flowers, leaves, hearts, birds, borders. Another approach is to trace around cutout patterns of simplified shapes, such as the rooster (opposite) or large heart or flower shapes, traced or cut out freehand. These shapes can then be filled in with decorative strokes, such as on the opposite rooster. In either case, to paint the motifs with acrylic colors, squeeze little dabs of paint around the rim of a palette or plate. Have a jar of water and a rag or paper towel handy for rinsing and wiping the brush whenever you change colors. Thin the paints to cream consistency as you use them by dipping your brush into water and then into the edge of the dab of paint, mixing the water and paint together in the center portion of the palette. Mix in white paint to lighten colors; add darker shades for less bright colors. Don't, however, be timid about using bright or lightened colors. Traditionally, reds, yellows, blues and greens were the ones most often used. With time they became naturally "antiqued." If you want an instant antique, then add a final antique glaze. Small cans with directions are available in paint stores. In any event, a final coat of shellac or varnish will protect your decorative painting.

Painting Folk Art Dough Clay Projects: If you don't have anything on which you'd like to experiment with painting, consider making an object from Dough Clay (see page 14) using one of the rooster patterns on the opposite page. Be sure to apply a base coat to the front, back and sides of any Dough Clay projects to ensure their durability. Or, if decorating onto unprimed dough, seal the finished object with shellac or varnish.

FOLK ART CUTOUTS

In a book covering the history and heritage of paper cuttings*, this art is said to have been practiced in China for fifteen centuries. There, paper cuttings have been used to brighten up the walls and windows of homes, particularly in the spring. Called "Happy Flowers," brightly-colored cutouts were pasted on windows and ceilings, added to lanterns, gift wrappings and even used to decorate cakes. From Germany, too, come paper cutting traditions begun in Middle Ages religious orders and spread, later, to the surrounding country folk. Religious scenes and symbols were the subjects most often cut, sometimes especially for a wedding or a baptism. When made in an attitude of prayer, they were considered a religious exercise—a contemplative focus of the mind, concentrated by the work of the hands as a symbol of spiritual significance was formed. And, from European country folk, came the tradition of the intricately cut "love letter"—the Valentine—a tradition which today accounts for the largest portion, after Christmas cards, of the six to seven billion greeting cards sold annually. Why not learn to make your own greeting cards and notepaper, too, while you practice the ancient folk art of paper cutting?

Happy Flower Cutout Notepaper: In the lower right of the opposite page is an example of a fold-and-cut flower glued to a note card made from white drawing paper. The flower was cut from the type of lick-and-stick gummed paper that comes in packages of as-

sorted colors. Other papers such as Origami paper or plain-colored wrapping paper can be used, as can lightweight construction paper.

Step One: For the actual note card cut a rectangle of drawing paper into a piece at least 5" x 7". 3½" x 5" is the standard minimum size envelope allowed to be mailed without a surcharge. Fold this in half and set aside.

Step Two: For the flower, cut a square the same size or slightly smaller than the folded card *(Step One)*. Fold the square in half, see below, (a) then in quarters, (b) and into eighths, (c) round and cut off the longer tip of the eight-fold (d).

Step Three: Next, cut into the eight-fold as shown (e), cutting away some areas (shown shaded) and being careful to leave a network of paper intact so that when unfolded the design holds together.

Step Four: To glue the cutout to the note card: position and hold half of the design in place with the fingers of one hand while lifting the other half with your thumb; to the back of the cutout, apply very small dots of white glue, or brush on rubber cement, or, if using gummed paper, moisten the raised half with a wet cotton-tipped toothpick. Smooth the design in place and repeat on the other half.

Making Envelopes: Save different sizes of envelopes that come in the mail. Carefully take them apart and use these for patterns to make envelopes to match note cards.

*The Paper Cut-Out Design Book, by Ramona Jablonski, Stemmer House, 1976.

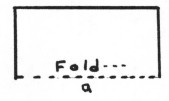
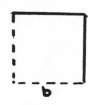

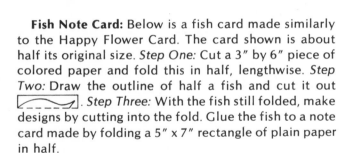

Fish Note Card: Below is a fish card made similarly to the Happy Flower Card. The card shown is about half its original size. *Step One:* Cut a 3" by 6" piece of colored paper and fold this in half, lengthwise. *Step Two:* Draw the outline of half a fish and cut it out. *Step Three:* With the fish still folded, make designs by cutting into the fold. Glue the fish to a note card made by folding a 5" x 7" rectangle of plain paper in half.

Heart and Tree Cards: Cards similar to those shown to the left below are made as follows: *Step One:* From a folded piece of paper, cut a simple shape such as a heart or tree. This is your pattern. *Step Two:* Draw around the pattern onto a piece of plain white paper. Set this aside. *Step Three:* From colored gummed papers, cut out folk art motifs—wavy lines, zigzags, triangles, circles (for these use a paper punch). *Step Four:* Glue the gummed paper cutouts to the set aside paper *(Step Two)*. Let the cutouts extend out beyond the outlined shape. *Step Five:* Reposition the pattern from *Step One* on top of the glued, gummed-paper motifs. Again, trace around the pattern and cut it out. *Step Six:* Glue the motif-decorated, cutout shape onto an appropriately-sized card. By extending the cutouts beyond the outlined shape and then reoutlining and cutting through the gummed paper shapes, the result is a sharp-edged "printed" effect. You have made a fancy-looking card with only paper, pencil and scissors.

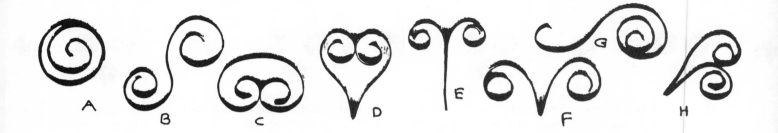

QUILLING—ANOTHER ANCIENT FOLK ART

Quilling is one of the art forms mentioned previously as being based entirely on the spiral motif. And, unlike working with wrought iron—which is impractical for most of us, and intricate silver or gold work—which is unaffordable, this is a folk craft anyone can do. Furthermore, the cost of the materials, if anything, is negligible—miscellaneous paper scraps and lightweight cardboard discards. The necessary tools are standard household equipment—scissors, a utility knife, a ruler, white glue, straight pins, and one other thing—a toothpick. Originally, a feather quill—thus the name *Quilling*—was used to form narrow paper strips into spiral and scroll designs.

As it happens, quilling has an interesting religious history. It is said to have originated during the Renaissance in the 15th Century in Italy when Italian nuns recreated biblical scenes and symbols with delicate, paper-filigree work. These were often used to decorate church and convent walls. The paper strips were trimmed from old books, and, as you can imagine, gilt-edged books were particularly prized. However, the more ordinary, plain-edged strips were often dyed for unusually beautiful and symbolically-meaningful decorations.

Preparing to Quill: The variations of the spiral learned on page 9 are the same component shapes as the quilling projects on this and other pages later in this book. They are shown above: A - the spiral; B - the **S** scroll; C - the curved scroll; D - the heart scroll; E -the closed **V**; F - the open **V**; G - the wave scroll; and H - the quote scroll.

A—the spiral—is most often closed with a tiny dab of glue on the outer edge. Its size depends on how tightly it is quilled and from how long a strip. E—the closed **V**—is normally glued closed.

The easiest procedure for quilling is to cut a pin board from a corrugated cardboard box, then to make a rough sketch on white paper of a design to be quilled. Place the sketch on the cardboard. Over it, place a piece of waxed paper. Secure sketch and waxed paper to the cardboard with straight pins.

Next, estimate the number of each separate quilled shapes you will need. Make these according to the directions below. An empty egg carton is a good way to keep the different shapes separate.

An important thing to remember is that no two people quill in the same way. The directions here are guidelines to get you started. You will soon learn the feel and the effect of tightly or loosely forming the

quills from long or short strips and from different weights of paper and lightweight cardboards. The fish to the right is an example of quilling from lightweight cardboard—about the weight of the cover of this book. The snowflakes on page 25 were formed from paper approximately the quality and weight of the inside pages of this book.

How to Quill *Step One:* Cut 1/8″ strips of white, black or colored paper into lengths as long as your paper allows. Keep your strips as close to the 1/8″ width as possible. Individual white strips can be colored with felt pens before they are quilled. Place each strip on a piece of newspaper and run the pen along one side; turn it and repeat. It is also possible to purchase precut quilling strips at some hobby and stationery shops.

Step Two: Using a round toothpick, moisten (I lick) the end of a strip, work it around the toothpick and roll it between thumb and index finger. All the shapes shown above were made from 4″ lengths. To make a plain scroll (A), roll the entire length of a strip. Then, close it with a very small dab of glue. A toothpick dipped into a small pool of white glue works best for me. How much you allow your spiral to expand will determine the size and density of the spiral. For a very loose spiral (as well as for other shapes) you may even need to pull the toothpick through the spiral to help it expand, and then to reshape it with your fingers to the size you want. The other shapes are formed, first from one end, then from the other end. In some cases, (D, E, F, and H), the strip is first bent into two halves. A bit of glue is put on the tip of E in order to close the **V**. The height of this shape is dependent on how many rounds the tips are quilled: ᕦ ᕦ ᕦ Practice making a few of each of the quilling shapes until you get the feel of it.

Step Three: When you have a specific quilling design in mind, place your rough sketch of it on the pin board under waxed paper and arrange your quilled shapes on it, stick-pinning the shapes to hold them in place temporarily.

Step Four: Connect the individual quill pieces with small dots of white glue wherever their sides touch. Be very sparing with the glue.

Step Five: Allow the glue to dry for at least one hour, then peel the design off the waxed paper and hang as an ornament, a mobile, or use it as a design on a wall.

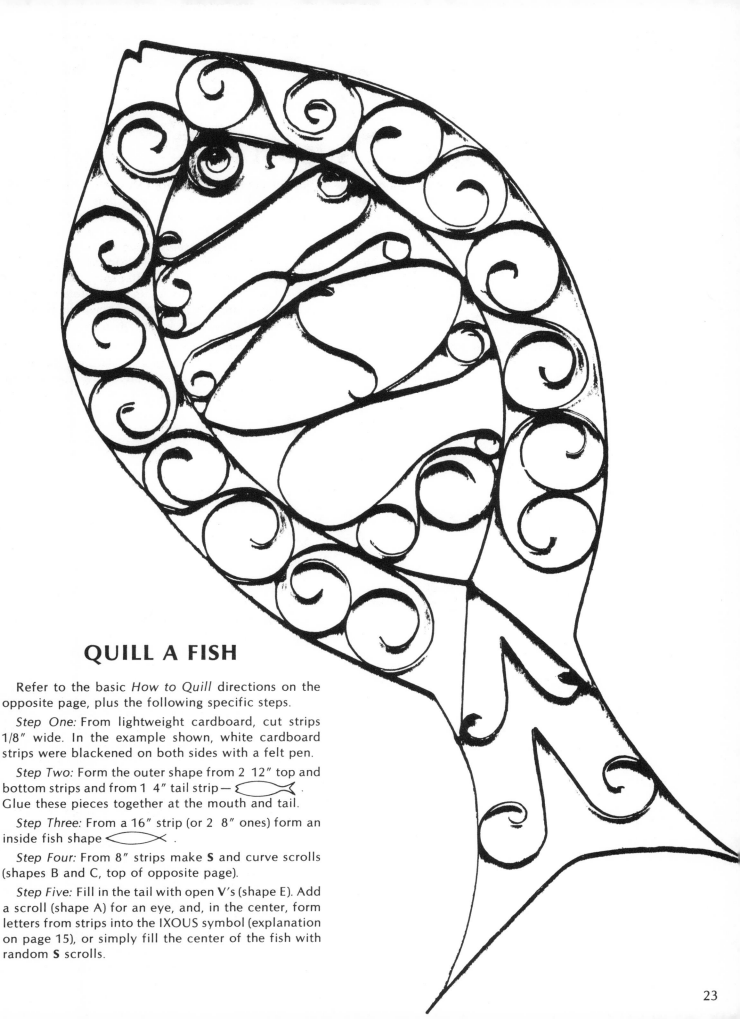

QUILL A FISH

Refer to the basic *How to Quill* directions on the opposite page, plus the following specific steps.

Step One: From lightweight cardboard, cut strips 1/8" wide. In the example shown, white cardboard strips were blackened on both sides with a felt pen.

Step Two: Form the outer shape from 2 12" top and bottom strips and from 1 4" tail strip — Glue these pieces together at the mouth and tail.

Step Three: From a 16" strip (or 2 8" ones) form an inside fish shape.

Step Four: From 8" strips make **S** and curve scrolls (shapes B and C, top of opposite page).

Step Five: Fill in the tail with open **V**'s (shape E). Add a scroll (shape A) for an eye, and, in the center, form letters from strips into the IXOUS symbol (explanation on page 15), or simply fill the center of the fish with random **S** scrolls.

QUILLING SNOWFLAKES

The snowflakes on the facing page may be hung in a window from different lengths of thread. There, from both inside and outside, they add a touch of beauty while being a reminder of the infinite variety of creation and the Creator who assures us that even the hairs of our heads are numbered and known to him.

By the time you have made the four snowflakes for which directions are given, you will know how easily you can make countless, each-one-different snowflakes that you design as you go along. A design guide will greatly facilitate the mechanical part of the arranging and gluing. But don't forget those "Open Sesame" words from the Folk Artist's Tool Kit: *Combine—Vary —Group—Rotate.*

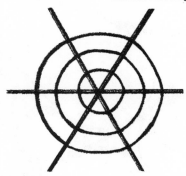

Making a Design Guide: On a sheet of white paper, draw a circle about 6" in diameter. (Use a compass or trace around a saucer.) Inside this circle, draw 2 smaller circles. Here you can use large and small jar lids in lieu of a compass. Next, divide through the circles into six, equal, pie-piece sections. On a protractor, this would be at 0°, 60°, and 120°, but your eye will probably be close enough. Place this guide on a pin board (described on page 22). Cover with wax paper. Secure both in place with straight pins.

Cutting the Quill Strips: All of the snowflakes here are made from 4" long, 1/8" wide strips of medium weight, white paper. Cut strips as long as your paper allows, then cut into 4" lengths.

Quilling the Snowflakes: These directions are for making snowflakes pictured in their actual sizes on the opposite page. Each one is made by assembling two or three of the basic quilling shapes (shown at the top of this page), and then repeating the assembly six times for the six "spokes" of the snowflakes. Refer to the *How to Quill* directions on page 22. Then proceed as follows:

Snowflake #1 *Step One:* From the 4" strips, make 6 spirals (A), gluing each of these closed. Also, make 6 **S** scrolls (B). *Step Two:* Arrange the spirals in a circle,

using the center circle of your Design Guide as an aid. Secure these to the board with pins. Now, with a toothpick, place a dot of glue between each spiral to connect them. You can probably manage this with the pins in place. *Step Three:* Arrange the 6 **S** scrolls, one going out from each of the spirals in the center circle. Connect the **S** scrolls to the center spirals with dots of glue. Allow the glue to dry for an hour before removing the pins and carefully peeling the snowflake from the wax paper. Hang from a length of thread.

Snowflake #2 *Step One:* Quill 6 quote scrolls (H) and 6 wave scrolls (G). *Step Two:* Arrange the quote shapes and glue them as in *Step Two* above. **Step Three:** Arrange the wave scrolls around the circle of

quotes and connect them with dots of glue. Allow to dry and remove as above.

Snowflake #3 *Step One:* Make 18 closed V's (E), quilling 6 of them short, 6 medium length, and 6 long. Refer to page 22, *How to Quill—Step Two.* In addition to the closed V's, the lower parts of which should be glued closed, also quill one spiral (A). *Step Two:* Place the spiral in the center of the Design Guide and arrange the short V's around this, securing with pins, and gluing together at touching points. *Step Three:* Join the 6 medium V's to the tops of the center V's. *Step Four:* Add the long V's to the tops of the medium ones. Now proceed as in the last part of *Step Three* of *Snowflake #1.*

Snowflake #4: Follow *Steps One* through *Three* for *Snowflake #1.* Then make 6 long closed V's and 6 medium closed V's. First, join the tips of the long V's to the center circle between the wave scrolls. Next, add the medium V's to the long ones, gluing the scrolled tops of each together. Proceed as above.

On Your Own: Quill a number of each of the basic shapes. Keep the different shapes separated in an egg carton. On one of the pie sections of the Design Guide make an arrangement of several of the shapes. Glue them together and repeat for the snowflake's other five points.

3

2

4

1

25

Part III — Introduction

ADDING COLOR AND MEANING TO THE SPECIAL DAYS AND SEASONS OF THE CHRISTIAN YEAR

Without a doubt, among the happiest and most rewarding activities of our family were the times we spent making our folk art Christmas decorations. Well, I'm not sure my husband Bob actually made any of the decorations. In those days, he was still claiming any artistic bent he might have had as a child had been irreparably inhibited. But he did make trips to the library to search out the meaning of some both usual and unusual Christmas symbols. And, when it came to putting up the tree, how particular he was to choose just the right tree! Such joy he took in supervising the placement of those decorations—original decorations created by his children's own hands.

The result of our activities was the establishment of some traditions of our own, and the creation of some family "heirlooms." It helped develop in each of us a pattern of wanting our lives to be rich, not in things, but in essential meanings. And it taught our children that Christmas decorations are not meaningless baubles you buy, but meaningful symbols you make. I became aware of the impact this activity had made on our children's lives when our oldest son was married and asked for his share of the family Christmas decorations: some of the delicately-crocheted snowflakes my Aunt Myra had made; several of the one-of-a-kind ornaments Bob's sister Ellie had created, "And please don't forget some of the folk art ones," he added wistfully.

Traditionally, the practice of Folk Art has been a family affair, blending and melding with the everyday life and work of a family. For our family, it has been a way by which the symbols and celebrations of our Christian faith have become integrated meaningfully into our life as a family. As a Church school teacher, I have appreciated the opportunities it offers for encouraging creativity while carrying out specific projects related to the Scriptures and to the Christian Year. As a Christian craftsperson, I have repeatedly experienced how folk art techniques offer unlimited possibilities for creatively expressing the praise and thankfulness one feels toward a Creator whose wonders are everywhere seen.

Always, the folk artist's inspiration has been closely tied to the rhythm of the seasons and to the celebrations of those seasons. In the solar seasons, there is an obvious inward/outward rhythm: the rest of winter; the awakening of spring; the growth and activity of summer; the practical harvest of autumn. In the Christian year, there is a similar rhythm by which faith and alignment with God evolves. The saints knew it and all who travel the spiritual path discover this rhythm of inner seasons. Advent is a reflective time, a time for discovering the meaning behind the symbols related to the coming of Christ into the world—into our individual lives. Then comes Christmas and its holiday—holy day—celebration. Epiphany follows, a time for becoming aware of others, of the mission—the expression—of Christ in our lives. Lent begins another cycle—an inward searching in preparation for rejoicing at Easter, followed by the Ascension and Pentecost and the outflowing of God's Spirit through our lives. On the following pages are folk art activities related to the revolving Christian seasons.

Bob, in his research, discovered that Renaissance artists had included particular birds and flowers in their pictorial histories of the birth and life of Christ because of the special meanings attached to these nature forms. The meaning of the birds we used are given on the opposite page. As for the special meaning of certain flowers, we discovered that rosemary, with its fragrant leaves and tiny long-lasting blue flowers, is said to be for remembrance and for the mother of the Christ Child, who kept the secrets concerning the holy birth hidden in her heart. We discovered also that the poinsettia, in Mexico, is known as the "Flower of the Holy Night," its star-shaped petals symbolizing the Light of the World. The evergreen holly is also considered holy, because its thorns and red berries foretell the Crucifixion. The white Christmas rose is said to depict the innocence of the Christ Child. We added bells to our tree, not only because their simple shapes were easily decorated, but to remind us of the ringing in of a new era of salvation for humankind.

The olive branch-bearing
DOVE—symbol of
the Prince of Peace

The noble-hunter
FALCON—emblematic of
the King of Kings

The lowly SPARROW
—herald of the humbly-
born Carpenter of
Nazareth

The high-flying
EAGLE—foretelling
the courage and
spiritual height
of Jesus Christ,
Saviour

The legendary-
immortal PEACOCK
—signifying the
eternal nature of
The Christ
Child

ADVENT-CHRISTMAS FOLK ART

Traditionally, Advent is a time to reflect upon the meaning of Christ's coming into the world and into our individual lives. The symbols of the Christian faith, passed along from one generation to another, are the bearers—the outward, visible signs—of inner, invisible realities. When Advent preparations for Christmas are made in thoughtful consideration of the meanings contained within the symbols of the holiday season, then it becomes a time for the deepening of faith and the giving to children the gift of faith—a gift more lasting than any of the others they may receive.

Bird, Flower and Bell Patterns: On a piece of tracing paper, draw around the patterns on this and the next three pages. Transfer the patterns to heavier paper or to cardboard and cut them out. For a layered effect on the birds, follow the bold outlines, making separate body and wing patterns.

Christmas Tree Decorations: Possibilities for decorating shapes made from these patterns are shown on page 27 and on the cover. Permanent decorations can be made using either of the Dough Clay recipes on page 14. Don't forget to insert a hairpin or paper clip in the top of each, or to make a hole to receive an ornament hanger. Wings and bodies can be cut separately and attached by moistening the clay where pieces overlap.

After the shapes are dried, baked, and cooled, they can be painted with acrylics (pages 16 through 18). A very simple method of decorating them, one especially suitable for children, is to use red, yellow, blue, and green felt pens and the Folk Artist's Tool Kit motifs beginning on page 6. Draw with the pens directly onto the hardened Dough Clay. Then seal the shapes with shellac or varnish according to Step Eight on page 14.

Decorated Christmas Cookies: In our family we use these same patterns to make and decorate ginger cookies. Besides hanging them on our tree, we give them to friends and neighbors on foil-covered, cardboard "trays" covered with see-through plastic wrap and accompanied by a card telling the symbolic meaning of the shapes.

Ginger Cookie Recipe: This is my German grandmother's recipe, the one my mother used to make Christmas tree cookies when I was young, and the one I use for the bird, flower, and bell shapes. I've never lacked help in making these cookies. The children—now Joseph and whatever grown ones are home for the holidays—always seem anxious to help roll them out, cut, and decorate them.

Cream 1 cup butter. Add 1 cup sugar. Then add 1 egg; 1 cup molasses; and 1 teaspoon soda dissolved in ½ cup hot water. Next, stir in the following sifted ingredients: 5 cups flour; ½ teaspoon cloves; 1 teaspoon each of nutmeg, cinnamon and ginger; ½ teaspoon salt.

Blend the ingredients thoroughly and chill in the refrigerator for several hours. Roll out on a floured board and, with the tip of a knife, cut around the patterns. Make a hole in the top of each cookie for hanging it on the tree. Transfer the cookies to an ungreased cookie sheet and bake in a moderate oven (350 degrees) for 8 to 10 minutes. Be careful that the oven isn't too hot so the edges of the shapes do not brown before the body is done. Cool on racks. Ice and decorate. These cookies will keep for several weeks. That is they would if they were not so tasty.

Icing the Cookies: In a small bowl beat until thick 1 egg white and 1 cup of powdered sugar. Add 1 teaspoon vanilla and 1 teaspoon water. Using a pastry brush or a clean paint brush, ice the top of each cookie and allow the icing to harden.

Decorating the Iced Cookies: Mix a few drops of food coloring with a teaspoon of water. Use a separate custard cup or sauce dish for each color. Paint folk art motifs on the iced cookies. Use a small, pointed, watercolor brush which has been thoroughly washed and rinsed and which you rinse thoroughly whenever you switch from one color to another. Or, wrap toothpick tips with bits of cotton, one for each color, and use these for "brushes." Put a string or thread through the holes in the tops of the cookies. If the holes have closed during baking or icing, use a threaded needle, piercing it through the cookie, cutting off a length of thread to tie it onto the tree.

The Flowers: Patterns for the flowers on the facing page can be cut freehand and be made any size. By using various folk art motifs, different Christmas flowers can be suggested. Some of the symbolic meanings of flowers are told on page 26.

EPIPHANY

The word Epiphany means "God manifested." It is a feast of the Christian Year that celebrates the arrival of the wise men in fulfillment of Isaiah's prophecy: "I will give you as a light to the nations" (Isaiah 9:6). These wise men were believed to have been Babylonian Magi, representative of the gentile nations of the world. Some say the star they followed was the five-pointed star associated with Babylon. Others hold that it was the six-pointed "Star of David." Still others argue that the Nativity Star was the elongated Star-Cross, suggesting not only the birth, but the mission, of the Christ. In any event, the Epiphany Star is a good example of how geometric forms express abstract and theological concepts.

In the history of language, pictographs preceded alphabetical languages. Later, as written language developed, abstract thinking processes accelerated. Now the need was to simplify concepts and distill essential meanings. The use of geometric and pictographic signs and symbols returned on a new and higher level. For example, a triangle came to stand for the theological meanings of the Trinity, and a circle denoted the eternality of God. Similarly, monograms came to represent the different theological "faces" of Jesus. One example of this is the Alpha and Omega sign: $A \Omega$. In Revelation, Jesus is described as "the Alpha and the Omega" (Rev. 1:8). In this case, the symbol is in words—words that illuminate other similar scriptural statements about Jesus Christ: He is the invisible God made visible (Col. 1:15); He is the same yesterday, today, and forever (Heb. 13:8). More words could be said describing just this Alpha-Omega aspect of Jesus' nature, but in the symbols, $A \Omega$, it is expressed on the feeling and intuitive levels of understanding. You don't have to be a theologian to grasp the essential meaning behind a symbol. You sense, you intuit, the magnitude of meaning behind the symbol. The power of symbols and their function in both art and religion is their ability to say more than is possible with words, and to say it to deeper-than-conscious levels. *Symbols help human minds understand and express divine things.* Creating symbolic folk art is an extraordinarily-effective way of developing the intuitive and spiritual capacities as well as the creative potentials in children and grownups alike.

In folk art traditions, signs and symbols have played important roles. The oldest symbolic monogram for Christ and the one most widely-used by the early church was the $\times$. The I is the equivalent of our letter "J"—for Jesus. The $\times$ is for Ch—as in Christ and as in the abbreviation Xmas. These same letters also form a geometric pattern—the six-spoked hexagon—that is pregnant with meaning. In nature, the hexagon is the structural basis of the snow crystal. From the countless microscopic photos studied to date, no two have been found to be alike. This fact is attributed to the variables of temperature, moisture, and air currents. Yet every snowflake is based on the unvariable hexagonal theme. Moreover, this same geometric pattern is the basis for the Star of David ✡, which is to the Hebraic religion what the Cross is to the Christian religion. A synthesis of the $\times$ monogram and the $\dagger$ cross forms the Star-Cross $\ast$. The symbolic statement here is that as the Star of David is incorporated into the Star-Cross so the Old Testament is fulfilled in the New Testament accounts of the Incarnation, Crucifixion, and Resurrection of Jesus.

A good example of geometric folk art is found in the *Barn Stars* of the Pennsylvania Dutch. In recent years, these designs have been labeled *Hex Signs,* which, according to a leading Pennsylvania Dutch authority, is wrong. Their originators called them Barn Stars and brought this tradition from earlier European religious designs. Barn Stars were made by outlining circles on barns with the aid of six-foot-long wooden compasses. The circles then were divided into segments which were filled with repeat motifs based on the same three geometric shapes—the circle, square and triangle—Folk Artist's Tool Kit, page 5. Most frequent divisions were into sixths and multiplications of six (twelve and twenty-four). These Barn Stars had the same geometric pattern for their basis as the $\times$ monogram within a circle, for eternity ⊗ —"Jesus Christ the same yesterday, today and forever" (Heb. 13:8). The next most common Barn Star designs were circles divided into eight segments. The addition of a cross bar changed the hexagonal pattern into the Star-Cross octagonal pattern. From these basic themes countless variations of stars were elaborated.

In mislabeling Barn Stars as Hex Signs, their purpose was distorted into superstition. If, however, the designs originally were intended for the purpose of consecrating even their barns to God's purposes, and of committing them to God's protection, then the attitude was not superstitious but truly spiritual. In the one case, the Barn Stars would be a sign of fear; in the other, a symbol of trust and faith. In contemporary folk art, too, it is the attitude of the one creating and using a design that determines whether it is a sign of fear or a symbol of faith. In making the Star Pendants on the facing page, assume an attitude of reverence. This is far more important than striving for artistic perfection. In fact, it is good to keep in mind that one of the marks of folk art is its imperfections, and that the highest function of folk art is to reach out spontaneously to God with an offering up of one's creative efforts for his purposes. This, like rain watering the earth, blesses with joy the soul of the folk artist.

Star Medallions: So, whether you are making a Barn Star six-feet in diameter or a two-and-a-half-inch Star Medallion, the designing process is the same. You are putting together geometric components and enclosing them within a circle. A good way to get the feel of creating geometric folk art designs is to take apart some traditional ones, separating them into their components and then reassembling them. From this procedure you will get the feel of how easy it is to make up variations. The star-border design on the opposite page is taken from a photograph of a detail from a 19th century Albanian embroidered piece. The star design in the border is adapted for one of the medallions on this page. First, the design was drawn to pinpoint its components:

Eight-pointed Star *Step One:* Draw a circle and divide it into eight pin shapes. Make dots at the center and outer points of each line and also halfway between the outer and center points. Figure **a** below. *Step Two:* Connect the dots to make two curved-squares. Figure **b**. *Step Three:* Now make the eight-pointed star design, omitting the guide lines and broadening the star by drawing it with parallel lines. Draw it so that one of the curved-squares appears to be on top of the other. Figure **c**. *Step Four:* Add a center four-leaf clover and radiating lines from the clover and the star. Figure **d**.

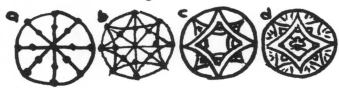

Six-pointed Star *Step One:* Draw a circle and divide it into six pie shapes with dots at outer points of each line. Connect the dots to make a six-pointed star. Figure **a** below. *Step Two:* Broaden the star with parallel lines so that one triangle appears superimposed over the other. Add a center three-leafed clover and radiating lines. Figure **b**.

Paper Cutout Medallions *Step One:* Cut a large circle from a piece of colored paper, using a compass, saucer or larger-sized plate. *Step Two:* Cut the design components out of differently-colored papers and assemble and glue them according to the Folk Art Cutout directions on page 20. *To Make the Eight-pointed Star* design (below, left) cut two squares of differently-colored paper approximately the same size as the background circle cutout in *Step One*. Fold these squares together in fourths, and cut them out as shown in figure **a** below. The center clover can be cut from a small folded-in-fourths square (figure **b**). Cut freehand radiating lines to suggest nails, and thus work further symbolic meaning into the design. *The Six-pointed Star* design (below, right) is cut from squares folded in half, as shown in figure **c** below, and the three-leafed clover is cut from a smaller folded-in-half square (figure **d**).

Dough Clay Star Medallions: With the components of Barn Stars understood, it is easy to transfer them to two-and-a-half inch Dough Clay circles in one of two ways. (1) The design lines can be impressed into the unhardened clay, freehand with a toothpick. Make a hole in the top of each circle so it can be hung from a thin, leather strip—available from hobby stores—and worn as a symbolically-meaningful piece of jewelry. To finish a medallion made according to this first method, follow *Step Seven* on page 14 for an antique look. (2) Another way to create a Dough Clay Medallion is to bake or air-harden the circle (see page 14) and then paint on a colorful, geometric design. (See Folk Art Painting, pages 16 through 18). The center design (below) is one of many Barn Star designs Joseph has made using a protractor. He then copies his design, painting it freehand onto a Dough Clay circle. With Joseph's many relatives, he "collects" birthday gift ideas such as these Barn Star Medallions.

LENT

In the history of religious art, no symbol has been more revered or had more variations and interpretations than the Cross. In museum collections, centuries-old folk art handicrafts depict the cross theme over and over—woven, embroidered, appliqued, and carved, painted onto wood, pottery, and leather. Today, thousands of crosses are being shaped and decorated by craftsmen for personal and corporate devotions.

Two basic, geometric designs comprise this vast array of crosses: the Greek Cross with four equal arms ✛ , and the Latin Cross with one, longer arm ✝ . The latter cross is the one most often associated with the Crucifixion. From these two basic types come numerous variations and interpretations. One, known as the St. Andrew's Cross, is ✕ shaped—the cross-shape on which Jesus' disciple is said to have been martyred.

Traditionally, Lent has been a time for focusing on the Cross, not only as a symbol of the Crucifixion but as a reminder of Jesus' words: "If anyone wishes to come after me, let him deny himself and take up his cross daily and follow me." Luke 9:23. Mystics and theologians alike have interpreted this to mean a moment-by-moment surrender of self to Christ in preparation for eternal life: "For what does it profit a man if he gains the whole world and loses or forfeits himself?" Luke 9:25. The purpose of making and placing crosses on the walls of homes as well as churches is twofold: as a reminder to keep thoughts and hearts centered on Christ and his Way of the Cross; and as an act of commitment, a consecration of the activities within the Cross-adorned walls to God's glory. In one ancient consecration ritual, 24 crosses were distributed equally throughout the building: three each to the inside and outside walls. The Pennsylvania Dutch Barn Stars may have been carrying out a similar ritual, taking it a step further in consecrating not only churches and homes but even barns to the glory of God. Not only must our higher —our church-life—selves be aligned with God, but our everyday—our home-life—selves must be, too; as must the third of our tripart nature, our more basically instinctual—our barn-life—selves. All three must, in preparation for living in the Kingdom of God, be committed to the transforming power of the Cross.

Researchers in the field of art and religion agree that the primary function of art is a striving that is more basic than intellectual—a feeling-level striving—to know God. This desire makes the folk artist's symbolic handicraft a work of prayer.

Folk art crosses can be made from the four craft methods detailed on earlier pages. The center cross on the facing page is quilled according to the directions for making snowflakes on pages 22 through 25, with this exception: Add a cross bar to the snowflake, Design Guide on page 24, and quill four rather than six spokes. For a Latin Cross, elongate one arm, and, if you wish, elaborate its base (as on the facing illustration). On the inside front cover is a very simply quilled Celtic Cross, made entirely from two quilling shapes —the scroll and the closed **V**.

The crosses on the opposite page numbered 1 through 7 were cut from 2" squares folded in eighths. Directions for making eight-folds for Folk Art Cutouts are given on page 20. The shaded areas of the diagrams below show what portions to cut away for the correspondingly-numbered result on the facing page.

Crosses numbered 8 through 10 (opposite) were cut from 2" by 3" eight-folded paper. In this case, think of a 2" by 3" rectangle as divided into two sections, into a 2" square and a 1" by 2" section ▢▢ . Fold the 2" square section the same as above, and simply allow the extra 1" section to extend (as shown in diagrams 8 through 10 below). For these crosses, too, cut away the shaded areas and unfold for the correspondingly-numbered results shown opposite. On the diagrams below, **x** marks the center of each cross.

All ten of the fold-and-cut crosses illustrated can be used as patterns for making Dough Clay pendants, as can many, many more cross variations of your own design. Again, as in other folk art projects, one idea leads to another, and another. Dough Clay directions are on page 14 and, if you have made the Barn Star Medallions on page 33, making Cross Pendants is a next, only slightly more difficult step.

Patterns for larger paper-cut crosses similarly can be made, and these decorated with openwork cutouts and/or builtup layers of variously-colored folk art motifs. (See Folk Art Cutouts on page 20.)

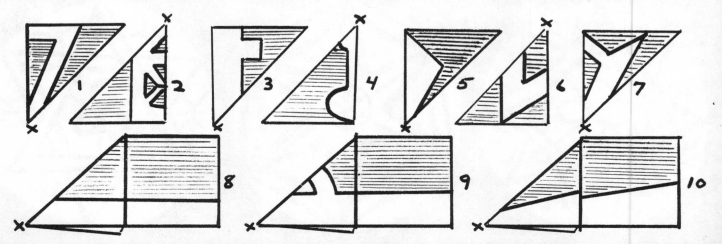

EASTER

The Flowering Tree of Hope

The folk artists of Early America based their hope for eternal life on Jesus' Resurrection victory. Tulips, lilies, and all flowers that bloom, die, and bloom again were symbolic of this hope. Not only was it a hope for eternal life but a belief that through Jesus, "the pioneer and perfector" of their faith (Hebrews 12:2) they could live victoriously in this life. Through his strength they could endure in suffering, and persevere in adversity. A witness to this belief was the often-repeated flowering tree theme in their art.

Flowering Tree Patterns: The patterns on this page, shown assembled on the opposite page and in color on the cover, are but one variation of the folk art, flowering-tree theme, sometimes called The Tree of Life.

Specific ideas on materials to use and techniques for cutting and adhering Folk Art Cutouts are on pages 20 and 21. In making the flowers, use a variety of contrasting colors, cutting each flower in duplicate and on the fold. Set aside one of the two cutout shapes and into the other (still on the fold) make openwork designs, being careful to leave the outer edges of the shape intact. Glue the openwork flower onto the contrasting, set-aside one. This is a simple way of achieving a variety of intricate-appearing flowers. As a final step, assemble tree and flowers and glue them onto a background, following the directions for *Step Four* on page 20.

Flowering trees can be made as large or as small as you wish—for wall hangings or for Easter greeting cards. To enlarge or reduce the patterns, study each one, noting the simplicity of its line and shape. Then, directly into once-folded paper, freehand cut stem (trunk), leaves and flowers. Assemble and adhere as above.

ASCENSION

One Christmas when my daughter Louisa was about four years old, she commented, "When Jesus was born the angels came out to say goodby." Ever since, when Ascension comes around forty days after Easter, I think of Louisa's angels, now rejoicing over Jesus' return.

Angels are one of the most popular folk art themes. They, like the wind that comes and goes to and from unknown places and realms, are said to be messengers of God, guardians of children (and the child spirit in each of us), and sentinels at such places as the east gate of Eden, the Easter morning tomb, and the scene of the Ascension, when they informed Jesus' disciples; "As he has left, so will he return" (Acts 1:11).

Folk art angels make thoughtful presents for newborn or young children, especially when accompanied by a scripture reference. The angel design opposite is simple enough in shape to be made easily from Dough Clay (page 14) and finished as suggested for the fish on page 15, or painted folk art style as detailed on pages 16 through 18.

PENTECOST

Pentecost is considered second to Easter in importance as a Christian Feast. Originally, it was the Jewish Feast of First Fruits and followed fifty days after the Passover Sheaf Offering. Later, the Pentecost celebration included commemoration of Moses' receiving the Law on Mount Sinai. Through the Law the Twelve Tribes of Israel were fused into one nation. For the early Christians, Pentecost, coming fifty days after Easter, was observed in honor of the descent of the Holy Spirit upon Jesus' followers waiting together in Jerusalem. Now, it was through Grace that twelve-plus-one-hundred (representing the earlier Twelve Tribes) were fused into one body — a Body of Believers to whom Jesus had promised to send a Comforter to empower and instruct them from within. This new Pentecost was seen as the beginning or the "first fruits" of the Christian Age. Today's Pentecostal and Charismatic movements identify with the original Pentecost and see the spiritual fruits of their lives as a "latter-day harvest."

The two primary symbols for the coming of the Holy Spirit, both in folk and in Renaissance art, are the dove, based on John 1:23, and the "cloven tongues like as of fire" (Acts 2:3). Flames are sometimes shown as luminous, rainbow-colored rays, or as forming a halo, indicating the Holy Spirit emanating from a person or from a symbol-concept such as the "Sacred Heart." When, however, flames are shown descending, they usually are "cloven"—in pairs—as in the scriptural Pentecost account. I once heard Agnes Sanford, author and teacher on the gifts of the Spirit, point out that in the Gospel recording of Jesus' baptism, it says the Holy Spirit descended as (in the shape of) a dove. She suggested this may have been a manifestation of spiritual power made visible and was similar to the Pentecost occurence. Her observation was how close in essential outlines were the wings of a descending dove and of "cloven" tongues of fire.

Light Circles: These humble folk art circles are "country cousins" to resplendent cathedral windows. Their component parts and how they are assembled are shown opposite. Symbolically, these circles demonstrate the same truth as a stained glass rose window: How God's Light—his Spirit—transforms lives. Held to a window, in the light, the circles show a remarkable change. All the colors will blend to form a new pattern, intricate and brillant. So it is with persons. The life of a human being may be ordinary, without purpose, without meaning. But, let the Light of God penetrate it, and that life becomes, as its source, full of beauty and joy.

Step One: Fold wax paper together to form 6½" squares. Outline a 6¼" circle, using a compass or saucer, and cut out the wax-paper circles. Allow four of these for each **Light Circle** to be made.

Step Two: Cut 6" squares of tissue paper from a wide assortment of *bright* colors. Fold and cut as shown in the figure drawings **a** through **d** on page 20.

Step Three: Cut into the folds as shown in figure **e** on page 20, cutting away some areas and being careful to leave a network of paper intact so that when unfolded the design will hold together. The kaleidoscopic patterns, as suggested on the facing page, can be varied and infinite as the forms of snowflakes. Let your only rule be: experiment and innovate and discover yet another new cutout pattern.

Step Four: Place the colored cutouts between the wax circles, first a wax circle, then a colored cutout, then wax, and so on, ending with a wax circle, as shown on the opposite page.

Step Five: Place the wax and tissue layers between sheets of plain paper, and press with a warm iron. The wax will weld the layers of tissue into a stiff translucent disc.

Step Six: Fasten each disc to a window with a small piece of double-stick cellophane tape, or hang several by thread from the ceiling, in front of a window, where light will catch, bring out, and blend their bright colors.

He gives Angels Charge over thee.

THE STAR-CROSS

There is, in the eight-directional Star-Cross, a message so broad as to cover all the events of the Incarnation. In composition, this symbol is a combination of the Latin Cross— † —the cross traditionally associated with the Crucifixion, and the St. Andrew's Cross— ✕ —the shape upon which Jesus' fisherman disciple is said to have died.

† ✕ ✳

In navigational terms, this same sign is referred to as the star-compass—pointing not only to the four cardinal directions but to the in between directions, too. As such, it evokes a sense of the all encompassing universality of Jesus the Christ—*his cosmic totality*. As a focus of devotion, the star shape of this symbol calls to mind the Nativity-Epiphany events. Its vertical-horizontal lines recall the Crucifixion. While the combined, radiating lines suggest light overcoming darkness—the Resurrection. Taken as a whole, this symbol broadcasts a call: "Come to the Cross." As a symbol-in-words, *Coming to the Cross* means accepting Christ's assurance that our sins, even our sinful natures, are forgiven—washed away by the *Blood of Calvary*. No longer need a person feel outcast and excluded. The Cross—all encompassing, all inclusive—says that because of it, all can come home to God and be embraced as beloved children of The Father.

To meditate upon a symbol in this way is to understand it on both head and heart level. To comprehend not only what the symbol stands for but also to relate to it on a feeling level is to make a connection with the Reality behind the symbol. There is a way of praying that involves head, heart and hands: meditating upon the meaning of a symbol; desiring to be in touch with the underlying reality of the symbol; and, with the hands, giving shape to the symbol. About such a way of praying Ecclesiasticus 38:39 has this to say: "And in his handicraft shall be his prayer." Understanding this, it is easier to appreciate the spiritual activity that was involved as members of cloistered orders in the Middle Ages sat quilling crosses and other religious symbols, and why it is that crafts made by folk artists the world over can go beyond being mere decoration to being messages of faith, hope and love. In a very real way, crosses, made by hands whose lives are committed to the Way of the Cross, can be vehicles of spiritual blessings. With these things in mind, here is one last head-heart-and-hand folk art exercise:

Quilling a Star Cross—The same directions apply here as those on page 24 for Quilling Snowflakes. Add a vertical line to the Design Guide given there, and instead of six arms quill eight. Depending on the size of the Star-Cross to be made, a larger piece of cardboard for a pinboard may be needed. If, as a starter, you would like to make one similar to the one shown opposite, the quilling shapes used (shown separately below) are listed below. After quilling this one you can make up any number of variations of all sizes. Give them as gifts, not just for Christmas but whenever you want to give a tangible sign of your concern and prayers for another.

From the center out: 1 loosely quilled spiral (A); 8 more-tightly quilled spirals; 8 heart scrolls (D); 24 spirals—large, small, loose and tight—to encircle the center. For the east and west arms: 2 closed **v** shapes (E); 1 curved scroll (C); 1 inverted closed **v**. For the north arm: 2 closed **v**'s; 1 curved scroll; 1 spiral; 1 inverted closed **v**. For the south arm: 2 closed **v**'s; 1 curved scroll; 1 spiral; 2 open **v**'s (F) place sideways; another spiral; another curved scroll; another spiral; and a closed **v**. For the in between arms: 2 closed **v**'s; 1 smaller open **v**; 1 small closed **v**.

For instructions on laying out a quilling design, gluing it together, and hanging it as an ornament or window decoration, refer to steps two and three for Snowflake #1 on page 24.

Another way of displaying a quilled Star-Cross is on a poster or cardboard backing. Choose a dark-colored poster board or paint a piece of cardboard a flat dark color. Cut the board into a diamond or rectangular shape slightly larger than the finished symbol. At each outer point of the design and in the center invisibly mount it to the backing with a needle and white thread. Bring the needle through from the back as close to the design as possible; loop it over a section of the design; push the needle back through, again as close to the design as possible; tie and cut the ends of the thread.

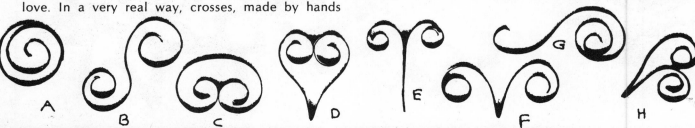